the

by James Gr.

SEPT NAMES INCLUDE:

Baxter	**Brown**
Bell	**MacNamell**

the
MACMILLANS

MOTTO: I learn to succour the distressed

CREST: A pair of hands brandishing a two handed sword

PLANT BADGE: Holly seedlings

TERRITORY: Knapdale, Lochaber, part of Galloway

Tartan featured on the cover is Macmillan, HTG Ancient

Published by Lang Syne Publishers Ltd. Clydeway Centre,
45 Finnieston Street, Glasgow G3 8JU
Printed by Thomson Litho, East Kilbride
Design by The Quick Brown Fox Company (Scotland) Limited

I.S.B.N. 185 217 061-1

Reprinted 2007

THE ORIGINS OF THE CLAN SYSTEM

by Rennie McOwan

The original Scottish clans of the Highlands and the great families of the Lowlands and Borders were gatherings of families, relatives, allies and neighbours for mutual protection against rivals or invaders.

Scotland experienced invasion from the

Vikings, the Romans and English armies from the south.

The Norman invasion of what is now England also had an influence on land-holding in Scotland. Some of these invaders stayed on and in time became 'Scottish'.

The word clan derives from the Gaelic language term 'clann', meaning children, and it was first used many centuries ago as communities were formed around tribal lands in glens and mountain fastnesses.

The format of clans changed over the centuries, but at its best the chief and his family held the land on behalf of all, like trustees, and the ordinary clansmen and women believed they had a blood relationship with the founder of their clan.

There were two way duties and obligations.

An inadequate chief could be deposed and replaced by someone of greater ability.

Clan people had an immense pride in race.

Their relationship with the chief was like adult children to a father and they had a real dignity.

The concept of clanship is very old and a more feudal notion of authority gradually crept in.

Pictland, for instance, was divided into seven principalities ruled by feudal leaders who were the strongest and most charismatic leaders of their particular groups.

By the 6th century the 'British' kingdoms of Strathclyde, Lothian and Celtic Dalriada (Argyll) had emerged and Scotland, as one nation began to take shape in the time of King Kenneth MacAlpin.

Some chiefs claimed descent from ancient kings which may not have been accurate in every case.

By the 12th and 13th centuries the clans and families were more strongly brought under the central control of Scottish monarchs.

Lands were awarded and administered more and more under royal favour, yet the power of the area clan chiefs was still very great.

The long wars to ensure Scotland's independence against the expansionist ideas of English monarchs extended the influence of some clans and reduced the lands of others.

Those who supported Scotland's greatest king, Robert the Bruce, were awarded the territories of the families who had opposed his claim to the Scottish throne.

In the Scottish Borders country – the notorious Debatable Lands – the great families built up a ferocious reputation for providing warlike men accustomed to raiding into England and occasionally fighting one another.

Chiefs had the power to dispense justice and to confiscate lands and clan warfare produced a society where martial virtues – courage, hardiness, tenacity – were greatly admired.

Gradually the relationship between the clans and the Crown became strained as Scottish monarchs became more orientated to life in the Lowlands and, on occasions, towards England.

The Highland clans spoke a different language, Gaelic, whereas the language of

Lowland Scotland and the court was Scots and in more modern times, English.

Highlands dressed differently, had different customs, and their wild mountain land sometimes seemed almost foreign to people living in the Lowlands.

It must be emphasised that Gaelic culture was very rich and story-telling, poetry, piping, the clarsach (harp) and other music all flourished and were greatly respected.

Highland culture was different from other parts of Scotland but it was not inferior or less sophisticated.

Central Government, whether in Edinburgh or London, sometimes saw the Gaelic clans as a challenge to their authority and some sent expeditions into the Highlands and west to crush the power of the Lords of the Isles.

Nevertheless, when the 18th century Jacobite Risings came along the cause of the Stuarts was mainly supported by Highland clans.

The word Jacobite comes from the Latin for James – Jacobus.

They wanted to restore the exiled Stuarts to the throne of Britain.

The monarchies of Scotland and England became one in 1603 when King James VI of Scotland (1st of England) gained the English throne after Queen Elizabeth died.

The Union of Parliaments of Scotland and England, the Treaty of Union, took place in 1707.

Some Highland clans, of course, and Lowland families opposed the Jacobites and supported the incoming Hanoverians.

After the Jacobite cause finally went down at Culloden in 1746 a kind of ethnic cleansing took place. The power of the chiefs was curtailed.

Tartan and the pipes were banned in law.

Many emigrated, some because they wanted to, some because they were evicted by force.

In addition, many Highlanders left for the cities of the south to seek work.

Many of the clan lands became home to sheep and deer shooting estates.

But the warlike traditions of the clans and

the great Lowland and Border families lived on.

Their descendants fought bravely for freedom in two world wars.

Remember the men from whence you came, says the Gaelic proverb, and to that could be added the role of many heroic women.

The spirit of the clan, of having roots, whether Highland or Lowland, means much to thousands of people.

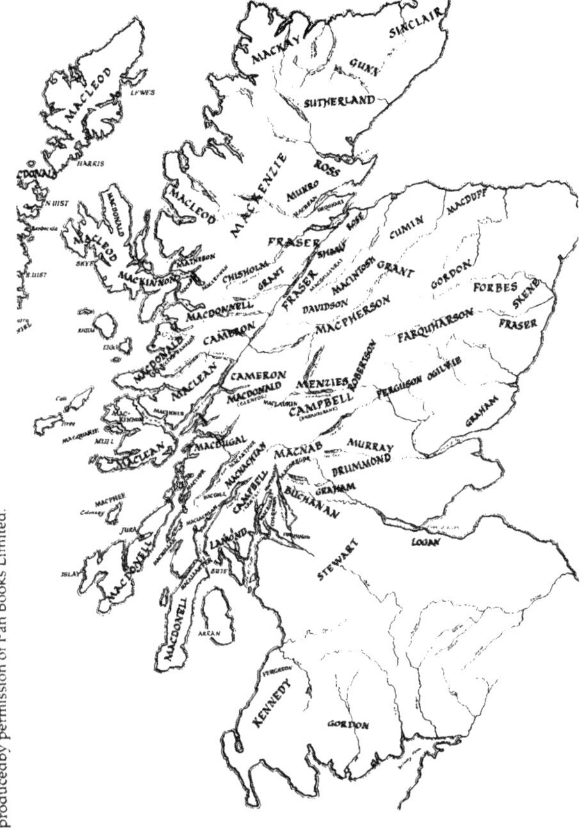

A map of the Clans Homelands.

Chapter One:
The Men of God

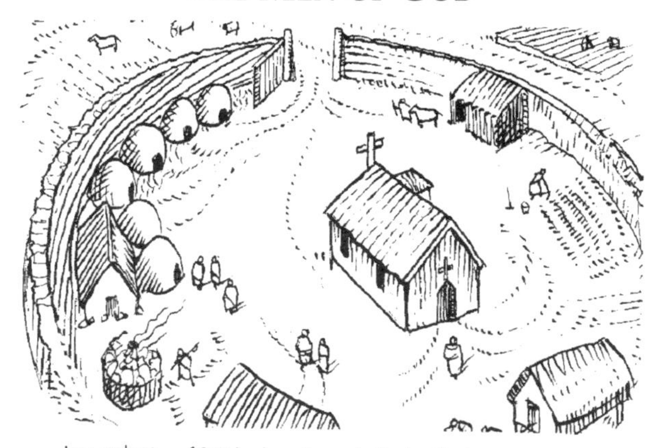

Iona at the time of St Columba – the monks lived in "beehive"-type cells.

The Macmillans, like the Macphersons ("sons of the parson") and the Macnabs ("sons of the abbot"), have an ecclesiastical origin.

In Gaelic, maol means bald or tonsured, so MacMhaollein is "son of the bald or tonsured one". Baldness in olden days was common, so to name a family after such an ordinary feature would have been unlikely.

However, ordination into the priesthood was much more unusual, so the ecclesiastical origin seems the likelier.

The name is therefore ancient, as the tonsured one in question would have been a monk of the Columban church. This was named after St Columba, who founded it on Iona in the 6th century.

The Columban church predates Roman Catholicism in Scotland, and prized celibacy as a virtue within its priesthood. However, it was never insisted upon, and many priests married.

This tonsure was not the one we know today, where the crown of the head is shaved, leaving a fringe of hair. It consisted of shaving the hair in front of a line drawn across the skull from ear to ear.

It was called St John's tonsure, and was the subject of a great argument between the Columban church and the Roman Catholic church in the 7th and 8th centuries. Eventually Roman practice prevailed.

The first instance we have of a name sounding like Macmillan is also ecclesiastical. Within The Book of Deer, written by Columban monks in the ninth century, is a list of local clans and families. One of the names is Maolan.

Deer was a monastery at Old Deer in Aberdeenshire, and it is thought that these are the lands where the Macmillans originally came from.

In some areas of Argyll the Macmillans were called Na Belaich, "the Bells". The word "beld" means bald in Scots, and here again we find a connection with the tonsure.

Some people claim that the family is a sept of the Buchanans or Munros, or that they belong to Clan Chattan. Certainly there has always been a close relationship between the Macmillans and the Buchanans.

We will probably never know for certain how the Macmillans, the "sons of the bald or tonsured one", came into being all these years ago.

What we do know is that the clan

A kilted Macmillan arrives in Edinburgh with his wife to st

in the Capital after a long trek from the Highlands.

eventually spread, not just throughout the Highlands, but into the Lowlands as well.

The victorious clansman!

Chapter Two: Spreading the Seed

Whatever the origins of the clan, we know that by the 12th century they had settled around Loch Arkaig, north of Fort William. From there they established small colonies in Muir Lagan, Glen Spean, Caillie, Glen Urquhart and Lochaber.

These areas are close to Cameron territory, and the Macmillans of Lochaber in particular were loyal followers of Cameron of Lochiel, though occasional skirmishes between the two clans were not unknown.

In those days, the king had absolute power, and he could move people about at will. In the 12th century, Malcolm 1V uprooted most of the original Loch Arkaig Macmillans and resettled them near Loch Tay in Perthshire.

The colony became known as Mac-na-Maoile, and its lands included Ben Lawers. In the 14th century most were driven out once again, this time by members of the Chalmers family.

A skirmish between the Camerons and Macmillans.

Some went to Knapdale in Argyllshire, and some went to Galloway. The Knapdale Macmillans became a powerful family whose head was known as Macmillan Mòr of Knap.

On the shores of Loch Sween is Castle Sween, said to be one of the oldest stone castles in Scotland. It had been built by the MacSweens, though it was later owned by the Macneills.

Alexander Macmillan, in 1472, was the first of his family to occupy it. He gained the castle by inheritance. His father-in-law had been Hector Macneill, last keeper of the castle for the Macneills.

No doubt Archibald viewed Castle Sween as a fitting and permanent abode for someone who ruled such a thriving area. As we shall see, this was not to be.

Knapdale probably held ten times the population it does today. You can still see evidence of artistic endeavour in its old carved stones and monuments. This suggests not only the wealth to have them done, but a certain amount of leisure time.

One of the monuments is called Macmillan's Cross, which stands within the ruins of Kilmory Chapel. It was commissioned by Alexander Macmillan himself, and has an inscription in Latin to this effect.

It shows, on one side, the Crucifixion, with Mary on one side of the cross and St John on the other, holding the Gospel. This may be a deliberate reference to St John's tonsure.

On the other side is a Highland chief hunting a deer, and this chief could be Macmillan Mòr himself.

There's a tradition that the son of a Macmillan Mòr once slew a man in Knapdale, and fled back to Lochaber with some companions to place himself under the protection of Cameron of Lochiel.

Cameron did indeed offer him protection, and one of the companions subsequently returned to Argyll and established the Macmillans of Glenshira at the head of Loch Fyne.

Another interesting tale is told of one

Archibald Macmillan who sought sanctuary in the Campbell stronghold of Inveraray Castle after killing someone.

He changed clothes and hid in the kitchen, where he began to knead dough. His pursuers failed to recognise him, and Archibald made good his escape after they left.

He eventually settled in Glendarual, where his sons became known as Mac-baxtear, "son of the baker". "Mac" was eventually dropped, and the Baxter family, a sept of the Macmillans, was established.

The overlord in Knapdale was the Lord of The Isles - someone who was almost a king in his own right. The Lord at that time was John MacDonald.

In 1473 John forfeited Knapdale to James 111 when that monarch at last succeeded in asserting his rule on the west coast. The king, now in absolute control of the area, granted Knapdale and Castle Sween to Colin Campbell, 1st Earl of Argyll, in 1481.

Alexander therefore lost his castle, and in

Archibald Macmillan hid in the kitchen where he began to knead dough.

1645 it was burned and dismantled by Royalist forces led by Alexander MacDonald. However, the ruins have now been consolidated, and are open to the public.

It is said that the Macmillans' right to Knapdale was bestowed by the Lords of the Isles in writing, and that this writing was on a boulder.

There are many large, glacial boulders in Knapdale, some as big as a house. The site of this particular one was supposed to have been at the Point of Knap, though it has now long gone.

It was known as a choir Mhic Mhaoilan air a Chnap, or "Macmillan's title-deed to Knap". On it, in Gaelic, were the words, "While streams shall run and winds shall blow, Macmillan's right to Knap thou'lt know".

The family of Macmillan Mor eventually became extinct, and the chieftainship passed through various branches of the family.

Some Macmillans, in the meantime, spread south down to Kintyre, from where they crossed to Arran and eventually Ayrshire. None of these branches of the clan, nor those in Galloway, achieved any real influence. Some individual members, however, achieved greatness.

Most of the Macmillans who settled in Galloway did so within the Stewartry of Kirkcudbright. There they flourished, though not in the cohesive way they would have done in the Highlands. This was, after all, the Lowlands, and loyalty to clan was not as pronounced as it was further north.

The leading families in Galloway were the Macmillans of Brockloch and of Carsphairn. The latter hadn't in fact moved there from Perthshire, but from Knapdale.

The founder was a younger brother of one of the Macmillan Mòrs, and had no doubt been drawn to Galloway because of the Macmillans already settled there.

In those days, younger brothers had to make their own way in the world, and no doubt this particular Macmillan saw coming to Galloway as a way of seeking his fortune.

It was the Macmillans of Brockloch who were considered to be the chiefs of the Galloway Macmillans. In 1662, a member of the family was fined £360 – a crippling amount then – for refusing to acknowledge an episcopacy within the Church of Scotland.

Some of the Arran Macmillans, having crossed from Kintyre, then crossed to Ayrshire, and a few isolated settlements grew up there.

So the Macmillans were eventually to be found in many areas of Scotland. All, however, can look to the tonsured priest of Deer as the founder of the clan.

CHAPTER THREE:
THE GREAT AND THE GOOD

Macmillans have distinguished themselves in many fields of human endeavour. Claiming descent as they do from a priest, it isn't surprising that many of them became clerics and divines.

One was the Rev. Angus Macmillan, born at Glen Sannox in Arran. He lived through remarkable times on the island – called by some the "Arran Revival" – and played a large part in them.

Through the efforts of the Rev. Neil MacBride, minister at Kilmory to the south of the island, Arran in the early 1800s had been gripped by an evangelical fervour.

When MacBride died, it had been his wish that Macmillan succeed him. But the local landowner had no love of the evangelicals, and appointed a moderate, Dugald Crawford, to the pulpit.

The parishioners abandoned the church,

The parishoners abandoned the church and held services in the "Preaching Cave".

and instead held services in a cave on the shore, called the "Preaching Cave". They had no disagreement with the Church of Scotland just with the landowner and the new minister.

The church languished while the cave thrived. Then, in 1820, Crawford was drowned when a boat on which he was a passenger capsized. The landowner wisely appointed Angus Macmillan to the pulpit, and the congregation returned.

He soon gained the reputation of being an inspired preacher, and people flocked from Arran, Bute and the mainland to hear him.

He eventually left the Church of Scotland at the Disruption, taking his congregation with him. He was the first cleric ever to have a religious book printed in Gaelic.

Throughout Galloway there were many Macmillans who adhered to the National Covenant. One was the Rev. John Macmillan, born in Minnigaff in Galloway in 1669 and ordained at the age of 32.

Though the Killing Times had ended by then, he still gained a reputation as a great adherent of the Covenant. His followers were called "Macmillanites", and he himself was known as "the last of the Cameronians".

After his death in 1763, his personal communion vessel became a sort of Holy Grail, and was called "Macmillan's Cup". The unworthy were not allowed to look at it, and it was supposed to have the power to ward off the evil eye.

No doubt John, fervid Calvinist that he was, would have disapproved. His grave can still be seen at Dalserf churchyard in Lanarkshire.

Another Galloway Macmillan – but not a cleric – was Kirkpatrick Macmillan, inventor of the bicycle. He was born at Keir Mill in 1813, and in 1842 he set out on his historic bicycle trip to Glasgow.

In the Gorbals he knocked down and

slightly injured a young girl, and was charged by the police – the first traffic offence by a cyclist.

Two astute businessmen from the Macmillan clan were the founders of that great publishing empire which bears its name. They came from the Arran branch of the family.

Daniel was born in Corrie, and his younger brother Alexander, who eventually became the head of the company, was born in Irvine, Ayrshire.

The firm first set up in Cambridge, and then moved to London. In 1869 it opened a branch in New York.

From this publishing family came the most famous Macmillan of all – Harold Macmillan, prime minister of the United Kingdom from 1957 until 1963. He had the nickname of "Supermac", and eventually joined the House of Lords.

The Macmillans were never a powerful clan, unlike the Macdonalds or the Mcneills.

However, they did produce many great individuals. Some are remembered to this day for having played their part in our history.

Clansmen on a raiding mission.

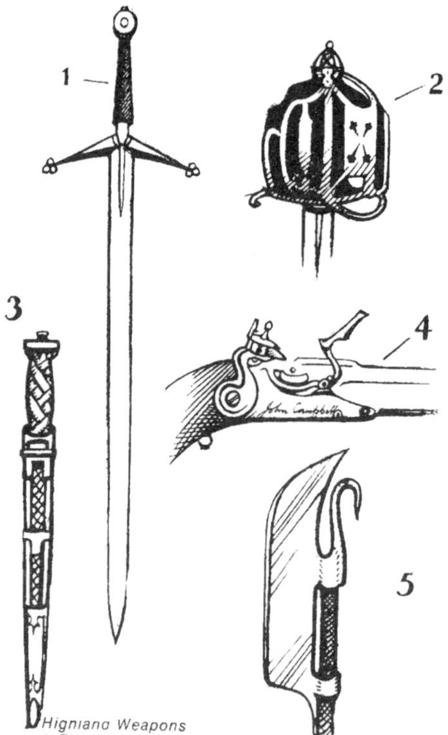

Highland Weapons
1. The Claymore or two-handed sword (Fifteenth or early Sixteenth century)
2. Basket hilt of Broadsword made in Stirling, 1716
3. Highland Dirk — Eighteenth century
4. Steel Pistol (detail) made in Doune
5. Head of Lochaber Axe as carried in the '45 and earlier.